The

ELDERSHIP

of the

Churches of Christ

A Study of Biblical Church Leadership

by

H. LEO BOLES

Editor of the *Gospel Advocate*

Charleston, AR:
COBB PUBLISHING
2023

Published in the United States of America by:
Cobb Publishing
www.CobbPublishing.com
Editor@CobbPublishing.com
479.747.8372

ISBN: 978-1-960858-01-6

Contents

INTRODUCTION 1

1: CHURCH GOVERNMENT 3

2: CHURCH GOVERNMENT— THE DIVINE FORM 9

3: CHURCH GOVERNMENT— THE ELDERSHIP 15

4: THE ELDERSHIP—HOW APPOINTED 21

5: THE ELDERSHIP—ITS PERPETUITY 27

6: THE ELDERSHIP— THE QUALIFICATIONS 31

7: THE ELDERSHIP—ITS DUTIES 37

8: THE ELDERSHIP AND PREACHERS 43

9: THE ELDERSHIP AND DISCIPLINE 49

10: THE ELDERSHIP—SOME QUESTIONS 55

INTRODUCTION

One of the major problems that confront the churches of Christ today is that of the eldership. Many congregations are inactive because they have not a Scriptural eldership; many others are divided over the question of elders; not a few have open division with opposing parties and factions because they have not sufficient leadership to guide the work and worship of the church. It is sad to think that so many of the churches of Christ are in such a deplorable condition that they cannot fill their mission.

The influence of a weak and divided church is such that the gospel of Christ is disregarded both by the church and the community where the church is located. Many of the churches of Christ are weak and unable to maintain the dignity and influence that a church of Christ ought to have in a community, because they do not understand the teaching of the New Testament on this vital question. A Scriptural eldership would give strength to the church and commend it to the community as a respectable group of worshipers. Churches everywhere ought to study this question and let the New Testament guide them in the selection of qualified men for this important work.

It is hoped that this study will help to clear up some questions and lead all into a fuller knowledge of the truth of God on this question. It is not claimed that these articles have exhausted a study of this important question, but it is claimed that they will help anyone who desires to know the will of God on this question. It is sent out with a prayer that it may fill this important mission.

H. Leo Boles

The Eldership of the Churches of Christ

Chapter One:
CHURCH GOVERNMENT

The church as God's divine institution should be studied from every angle that is revealed to us in the New Testament. We need to know all that is revealed concerning it, or God would not have revealed it to us. The fact that we find this institution, with its government, mission, and worship, in the New Testament, is sufficient evidence that we should study it. How does God govern his people today?

So far as we know, there was no divine government, except the family, until Moses gave the law to the children of Israel. The law of Moses was a provisional government. It was intended to be in force until another was given. How does God govern Christians today?

When the church was established on the first Pentecost after the ascension of Christ, the government of God's people was vested in the apostles. Inspired and miraculous helps were furnished the apostles. This was before the New Testament was given, and the government of the church at that time was primary and temporary. The apostles would not live always and the inspired men soon ceased. The permanent organization of the church grew up in the midst of the apostles, and it was to take the place of the apostolic rule. It is important that we give due attention to the government of the church during the days of the apostles; but we should not confuse the government of the church as directed by the New Testament with that which was directed by the personal supervision of the apostles and spiritually guided men. We are to study the perfected and permanent system of church government which began when the personally directed government by the apostles ceased. The church at Jerusalem is an example in its early stages of the government directed personally by the apostles.

"Church" is used in at least three different senses in the New Testament. First, it is used to include all the people of God and is synonymous with the kingdom of God on earth. Eph. 1:22; 3:10; 5:24 are instances of the church in the general sense. The church at Jerusalem, before others were established, was coextensive with the kingdom of God on earth. The second use of the word "church" is to include all the local congregations in a certain territory. "So the church throughout all Judea and Galilee and Samaria had peace, being edified" (Acts 9:31). In this instance "church" is used to include all of God's people in the territory named here. The third use of "church" is to denote the local congregation. 1 Cor. 1:2 is an example of "church" in the local sense. When we speak of church government, we mean the government of the local congregation. There is no organization of the church in the general sense on earth. Jesus is the Head, and there are no other officials. Neither is there any government or organization for a group of churches or churches in a certain province or country. The only church government that we have revealed in the New Testament is the government of the local congregation. God governs his people today through the local congregation. "Church" in the local sense means a group of baptized believers maintaining together the work and worship of God according to his revealed will. It means a group of Christians banded together to carry out the will of God on earth.

What is the relation of the local congregations to one another? They are all on equality before God. The size of the group or the number composing the group has nothing to do with determining the blessings that the church shall receive; neither will the number, great or small, prevent it from fulfilling its mission. The local congregations stand before God on equality. There is no *first* church in the sense of superiority or in the sense of receiving special blessings from God. No church is *central* in the sense of superiority or in the sense that other churches must depend upon the other church. There is no authority above the local church to which this church must bow in submission or pay homage, save that of the Lord Jesus Christ. All the local churches are organically separate from each other. There are no churches after the New Testament pattern whose organization makes it dependent on some other church. One church is independent of all others; that is, the local congregation can function and fill its mission without being dependent on any other congregation. It is independent in its organization, which means that its organic functioning can be done without the authority or assistance of any other congregation. All the local congregations are alike in organization. It matters not whether the church be in Japan or America, if it is patterned after the New Testament order, then it is like all other churches in organization that are patterned after the New Testament order. That is to say that whatever it takes to constitute the full and complete organization of one church, it takes that same organization to complete the organization of every other church. The churches are *one* in organization, as well as *one* in faith, in hope, in mission. Whatever may be the officers of one congregation that is patterned after the New Testament order, these officers will be found in every other congregation that follows the New Testament pattern. All the congregations have the same mission; all have the same order of worship; all are guided by the same law.

There are no organizations of churches. The only organization that is taught in the New Testament is the organization in the local congregation. There are no officers of any kind that may make laws or govern any group of churches. If the church follows the New Testament order, there will be no organization within the church that in any way hinders the free functioning of the church as ordained in the New Testament. The simple, independent functioning of the congregation must be left free to act as directed by the word of God. The only organization that the New Testament teaches is the organization of the local congregation with its elders and deacons. It was physically impossible for all Christians scattered over the earth to meet in the same place for worship; so it became necessary to localize the church for the convenience and development of its members. It was necessary for the church in the general sense to take the form of local congregations in order that God might govern the members of his body. We are impressed with the extreme simplicity which God has given to the local congregation. Whatever authority Christ left with the church was vested in the elders. There is no higher earthly authority in the churches than that found in the eldership, if authority it may be called.

The elders neither made the laws by which the church is to be governed, nor can they unmake these laws. The members of the body did not and cannot enact the laws by which the church of our Lord is to be governed. The elders, as servants of the church, must simply execute the law of Christ. They rule by the word of the Lord. They dare not assume any authority not delegated to them by the Lord. They must not manufacture any expedient nor substitute anything for the government of the church, save that which is found in the New Testament.

Chapter Two:
CHURCH GOVERNMENT—
THE DIVINE FORM

It has been noted and emphasized that the local congregations are all on an equality before God; that they are organically separate; that they are alike in organization; that they are independent of each other; and that all have the same work and mission. The activities of the church are various, and no one can estimate the importance of any phase of the work of the church. The Lord has not given any needless or non- essential work for the church to do. Furthermore, all the work that has been assigned to the church by the Lord must be done, if the church fulfills its mission. The elders of the congregation are to see that the church fulfills its mission. The eldership of the church must govern the church.

There are three theories devised by man for the government of religious people in the congregational capacity. This gives rise to three different forms of church government. They are mentioned here that the New Testament teaching of church government may stand out the more emphatic.

(1) Episcopal. This form of government recognizes three orders of the clergy—namely, deacons, who are generally young men serving a kind of apprenticeship; the priests, who have charge of parishes and exercise large powers; bishops, who have the oversight of a number of parishes. The entire district over which the bishop presides is known as a diocese. The Anglican Church, the Roman Catholic and Greek Catholic Churches are examples

of this form of church government. The Methodist Episcopal churches have a modified form of this kind of government.

(2) Presbyterial. This form is an attempt to reproduce the practices of the New Testament churches in which there was a plurality of elders. This form of government makes a distinction between the teaching elder, who is ordained as a minister and preacher, and the ruling elders, who are laymen selected for their ability in leadership. They together form the session and decide matters of ecclesiastical business. The Presbyterian Church is an example of this form of government.

(3) Congregational. This form of church government is based on the theory that each local church is a self-governing institution. All matters are settled by the vote of the members. The churches are loosely organized into associations, conventions, and congresses, but they retain complete independence. The Congregationalist and Baptist Churches are examples of this form of church government.

The New Testament churches are governed by neither of these forms. Sometimes—yea, frequently—it has been declared that the churches of Christ are "congregational in their government." This does not express clearly the New Testament order of church government. It is misleading to make such a statement, and much trouble has arisen from a misconception of the attempt to enforce or practice the "congregational form of government." All the authority for governing the church that Jesus left on earth has been vested in the eldership of the church. Paul said: "But we beseech you, brethren, to know them that labor among you, and are over you in the Lord, and admonish you; and to esteem them exceeding highly in love for their work's sake" (1 Thess. 5:12, 13). Again: "Let the elders that rule well be counted worthy of double honor, especially those who labor in the word and in teaching" (1 Tim. 5:17). And again: "Remember them that had the rule over you, men that spake unto you the word of God; and considering the issue of their life, imitate their faith" (Heb. 13:7). "Obey them that have the rule over you, and submit to them: for they watch in behalf of your souls, as they that shall give account; that they may do this with joy, and not with grief: for this were unprofitable for you" (Heb. 13:17). Other Scriptures could be quoted showing that the authority to govern God's people has been vested in the elders.

Elders are members of the congregation of which they are a part. Their authority does not go beyond the boundary or membership of their own congregation. No elder has any authority whatsoever over another congregation. The independence and autonomy of the church forbid one elder ruling over more than one congregation. Any system of church government that extends the authority of elders beyond the confines of their own congregation is contrary to the New Testament teaching and perverts God's order for the government of his people. All churches are organically separate and are governed by the same law and animated by the same spirit and seek the same end and are entrusted with the same power. If one elder or all the elders of a congregation had authority over other congregations, then the congregation of which that elder or elders are members would be superior to the church over which this elder or elders rule. This would destroy the independence and equality of the churches; it would nullify the autonomy of the local congregation.

Be it remembered that the eldership of the church has no power or authority to govern the Lord's people than that power or authority vested in them by the head of the church, which is the Lord. The authority of elders is restricted by the will of the Lord. Christ is "the chief Shepherd"; all elders are under-shepherds to him. The law or rule by which they are to discipline and guide the congregation is the New Testament. All elders mentioned in the New Testament had everywhere the same rank and the same work in the churches; they were all to receive the same honor. Elders in the New Testament are overseers *in* the church and are not to be lords *over* the church.

The Holy Spirit teaches that order should reign in the churches of Christ. Every member should function in its own place and should do its own work. The eldership is to see that such harmonious order prevails. "But let all things be done decently and in order" (1 Cor. 14:40). This implies that each church has control of its own affairs and that someone must superintend the work that all things may be done in order. If there be no leaders to guide in the activities of the church, confusion results. If the elders do not rule according to God's will, they are unfaithful to their trusts. If the congregation is not governed, then anarchy is the result. The Lord has ordained that the elders in the New Testament churches should rule, teach, and exercise discipline. All teaching of the congregation comes under the supervision of the eldership of the congregation. The elders are teachers, and they select teachers and supervise the teaching done by others. They are taught clearly in the word of God what should be taught, how it should be taught, and who should do the teaching. They are to rule with kindness and firmness, not lording it over God's people. They are to exercise discipline as the cases may demand. All of this is to be done for the building up of the body of Christ and the salvation of souls. The fearful responsibilities that rest upon elders should impel them to follow humbly and prayerfully the instruction found in the New Testament.

The Eldership of the Churches of Christ

Chapter Three:
CHURCH GOVERNMENT—
THE ELDERSHIP

All churches that follow the New Testament pattern are alike; they are alike in their organization. If it be found that one church had elders in it, we may reasonably infer, since all are alike in organization, that all other churches had elders. If a number of churches described in the New Testament had elders, we may conclude that all churches that follow the New Testament have elders.

It is very important that we study this question now, since there are some who claim that there should be no elders in the church now. Different positions or theories advanced by brethren have caused no little trouble with the people of God. I think that no one will deny that elders were placed in the churches in New Testament times, but some claim that elders ceased when inspired men ceased. We leave that question for future study, and now examine the proposition that all churches in New Testament times had elders.

The church at Jerusalem was the first to be organized; the word of the Lord was to go forth from Jerusalem. The first mention that we have of elders in the church is found in Acts 11:30. Here reference is made to elders in such a way that we infer that they had been in the church some time when this reference was made. There was a famine in the days of Claudius, and the disciples decided to send relief "unto the brethren that dwelt in Judea." They did this, "sending it to the elders by the hand of Barnabas and Saul." There were a number of churches in Judea at that

15

time. Jerusalem was the first place where a church was organized, and others were established in that province. This statement shows that these churches had elders. Again, we read that when Paul and Barnabas went to Jerusalem to lay before the brethren there the question about circumcising Gentile Christians, they went up to Jerusalem "unto the apostles and elders about this question" (Acts 15:2). The church was called together, "and the apostles and the elders were gathered together to consider of this matter" (Verse 6). We read further that after the decision was reached and they were ready to send word back to Antioch, "it seemed good to the apostles and the elders, with the whole church," to send a letter to the church at Antioch. (Verse 22). Again, reference is made to "the apostles and elders that were at Jerusalem" (Acts 16:4) in such a way as to show that there was a distinct class known as "elders" in the church at Jerusalem. We have no record when they were placed in the church, neither do we have any record as to how they were appointed in Jerusalem. The apostles were at Jerusalem, but there were also elders of the church there. We learn that when persecution came against the church at Jerusalem "they were all scattered abroad throughout the regions of Judea and Samaria, except the apostles" (Acts 8:1). Although the apostles resided at Jerusalem for a time, yet elders were needed in the church there. If elders were needed in the church at Jerusalem, where the apostles resided, may we not conclude logically that elders were needed in other churches?

We find that there were elders in the church at Ephesus. Paul from Miletus "sent to Ephesus, and called to him the elders of the church" (Acts 20:17). Paul made an address to the elders of the church at Ephesus, and speaks of them as "bishops" (Acts 20:28). They were to feed the flock and to take the oversight of it. They were bishops *in* the church and not lords *over* it. The church at Jerusalem and the church at Ephesus were two of the very large congregations mentioned in the New Testament. We read also of the elders of the church at Philippi. Paul included them in his letter to the church at Philippi. (Phil. 1:1). They were worthy of special mention.

Paul gave instructions to Titus and said: "For this cause left I thee in Crete, that thou shouldest set in order the things that were wanting, and appoint elders in every city, as I gave thee charge" (Tit. 1:5). Among the things that were lacking and for which Paul had left Titus in Crete was that he should "appoint elders in every city." We are to understand that these were elders of the church; that in every city where there was a church, he should appoint elders in that church. This emphasizes the fact that all the New Testament churches had elders. Again, we read that after Paul and Barnabas had preached the gospel and had established churches in many cities they returned and revisited those churches. "And when they had appointed for them elders in every church, and had prayed with fasting, they commended them to the Lord, on whom they had believed" (Acts 1:23). Here we have the positive statement that Paul and Barnabas "appointed for them elders in every church" where they had established a church. These Scriptures and incidents show that the church at Jerusalem had elders, that the churches in Judea had elders, that the churches at Ephesus and Philippi had elders, that Titus was instructed to "appoint elders in every city," and that Paul and Barnabas appointed "elders in every church." The proof that the New Testament churches had elders is clear, simple, positive, and accumulative. The question yet remains to be settled whether these elders were to be continued.

"Elder" is the name which we commonly give to this class of servants in the church. However, there are other names given to the same characters. For the use of the word "pastors," see Eph. 4:11; for the use of the word "teachers," see Eph. 4:11; for the use of the word "bishops," see Acts 20:28; for the use of the word "elders," see Acts 11:30; etc. The words "elder" and "overseer" refer to the same characters; they are used interchangeably; the qualifications required for elders and overseers are the same; and we do not read about two classes of men who are rulers over the congregation. We must conclude that they refer to one and the same class. Those who look after the flock are called "shepherds"; those who feed the flock are "shepherds"; "shepherds" and "pastors" mean the same thing; hence, "pastors," "overseers," "bishops," and "elders" must apply to the same class of men in the church. When these men have been appointed according to the New Testament order, and when they have been honored as the New Testament teaches that they should be, then the churches of Christ will be in much better condition to fill their mission than they have been heretofore. The Holy Spirit had a specific work for elders to do in the congregation. There was a specific work which should be done by those who were called in the New Testament "elders" in every church in New Testament times. It must follow that if churches today follow the New Testament order and the work outlined in the New Testament for a church, then there must be elders in every church today, or the New Testament churches are no patterns for churches today. If we are not to follow the New Testament in the organization of churches today, then why should we follow the New Testament example of work and worship?

Chapter Four:
THE ELDERSHIP—HOW APPOINTED

No one can ignore the divine organization of the church without rejecting God. It is as important to teach the divine organization of the church as it is to teach the doctrine and worship of the church. The divine organization of the church represents the wisdom and authority of God as much as the work and worship represents his will. The eldership has been depreciated and ignored until the elders themselves in many places do not respect their position. The church has in many places degenerated because of the lack of showing respect to the divine organization of the church. The elders have been superseded in their work, on the one hand, by the preacher, and their position ignored, and, on the other hand, by the members, until they have become almost useless appendages in the church. But we are to consider how elders are appointed.

Like many other questions pertaining to the eldership, there are diversities of opinions and conflicting theories about the appointment of elders. Some maintain that elders gradually are developed and grow into the position and work of elders. This position is not tenable. If one brother can grow and develop into an elder, why cannot many or all of the men so develop into elders? In large congregations there might be two or three dozen men who are capable in talent and suited in character to develop into elders. How would the congregation know just who the elders are, if they are gradually developed and assume the work of elders?

Others take the position that elders are appointed by prayer, fasting, and the laying on of hands. Those who maintain this position refer to Acts 6:1-6. This Scripture says nothing about elders or even deacons. It is generally understood that the six brethren mentioned in this Scripture were to serve as deacons; however, there is no statement in the text that shows that they were deacons. At any rate, this would show how the apostles appointed deacons, if it should be conceded that these were deacons. It would not teach how elders were appointed, and one would have to infer that elders were appointed in the same way that these deacons were appointed. The best that could be had from this Scripture is an inference. Again, Acts 13:1-3 is given to show that the ordination of elders in New Testament times was done by prayer, fasting, and the laying on of hands. But in this case elders were not ordained or appointed. Saul and Barnabas were sent out to the work which God had for them to do. They were not ordained as elders of the church at Antioch or anywhere else. This Scripture does not prove that *elders were appointed by the laying on of hands.* There is no Scripture that teaches that this was the way to appoint elders in the church.

Others claim that elders were elected by a vote of the church. They claim that a majority vote decides the question as to who shall serve as elders. In many instances those who claim that elders should be elected by majority vote claim that they should serve only a year, or, at most, three or four years, and that they should be retired and others elected to take their place. Such a position has no Scripture to sustain it. Not only is there no Scripture for electing elders by majority vote, but such a procedure would defeat the will of God. The writer does not care at this point to enter into a discussion of the "majority rule" of the church, neither the "election by majority vote" of elders. Suffice it to say here that such positions have no Scriptural authority. All the actions of the church must be the action of the entire church. The New Testament does not present any case where a part of the church can act one way and another part another way.

The New Testament always speaks of elders being "appointed" or "ordained." Nowhere do we read that elders were "elected." There is no method revealed in the New Testament for the selection or appointment of elders. We read that when Paul and Barnabas "had appointed for them elders in every church, and had prayed with fasting, they commended them to the Lord, on whom they had believed" (Acts 14:23). Again, Paul said to Titus: "For this cause left I thee in Crete, that thou shouldest set in order the things that were wanting, and appoint elders in every city, as I gave thee charge" (Tit. 1:5). There is no instruction given that teaches us how they were "appointed." The simple declaration is made that they were "appointed" or they were to be appointed. Since no Scripture teaches us *how* they were appointed, we are left free to appoint them in any way or by any method that does not violate a Scriptural principle and at the same time promotes Christian unity.

When God tells us *how* anything is to be done, then the manner in which it is done becomes a part of the will of God and must be followed or rebel against God; but when God does not tell *how* anything is to be done, then we are left free to use the best means and the best way that may be available which does not violate a principle, but promotes unity. The Holy Spirit has given the command that the gospel should be preached; no method of preaching has been revealed or commanded; hence, any method that does not violate a sacred principle, but at the same time promotes peace and harmony, that way or method may be used. Jesus commanded the apostles to "go . . . preach," but he did not tell them *how* to go; hence, they are left free to use any mode of travel that may be at their command. The important thing is to go and preach the gospel. So, when the Holy Spirit teaches that elders were to be appointed in every church, but gives no instruction as to *how* they were to be appointed, we are left free to act in that way that will best accomplish the end and promote the peace and harmony of the Lord's people. We cannot argue that elders should not be appointed because the New Testament does not teach us *how* to appoint them, any more than we could argue that we should not go and preach the gospel because the Lord did not tell us how to go, neither gave us any method by which the gospel should be preached.

Paul, in addressing the elders of the church at Ephesus, said: "Take heed unto yourselves, and to all the flock, in which the Holy Spirit hath made you bishops, to feed the church of the Lord which he purchased with his own blood" (Acts 20:28). Here we are told that the Holy Spirit had made them bishops, or elders, of the church at Ephesus. The Holy Spirit appointed elders then. To follow the teachings of the Holy Spirit now in appointing elders is the same as the Holy Spirit appointing them, just as any disciple who baptizes one into Christ Jesus is following the teachings of the Holy Spirit when that one is baptized by the authority of the Holy Spirit. When we meet for worship and follow the teachings of the Holy Spirit, our worship is directed by the Holy Spirit. So, when elders are appointed by the direction of the Holy Spirit, it is the Holy Spirit that appoints them. This ought to make all respect the appointment, and it emphasizes the responsibility of elders being faithful to the Holy Spirit.

The Eldership of the Churches of Christ

Chapter Five:
THE ELDERSHIP—ITS PERPETUITY

It is as important that we teach and contend for the New Testament order of the *organization* of the church as it is to teach and contend for the faith and worship of it. One phase of the New Testament is as important as another. No member of the church, and surely no one out of the church, today, has any authority to say that the doctrine, faith, and worship of the New Testament church are more important than the organization and discipline of the church. The Holy Spirit set up the church with certain definite organization. We should know that and should teach it. We should know just what the New Testament church has in its organization and discipline. No one denies the eldership of the New Testament church in the days of the apostles. All admit that there were "elders in every church." Some claim that the eldership belonged to the miraculous period of the church, and that it passed away with all spiritually gifted members. Those who make this claim deny the right of a church today having elders. They rebel against any class of men in the church who have been appointed or set apart as elders. They have caused much trouble and disturbance by their contention that the eldership ceased with the miraculous age of the church. If it be true that the eldership did cease then, these brethren are right in opposing the eldership. Their manner and method of opposition might be questioned. But if the New Testament teaches that the eldership ceased, they should stoutly contend with meekness and humility for the pattern of the permanent state of the New Testament church. But if the New Testament does not teach that the eldership ceased; if the New Testament teaches the permanent perpetuity of the eldership, then these brethren are radically wrong and are in open rebellion against God's order.

The church is "a body"; it has many members. This implies *organization.* "For even as we have many members in one body, and all the members have not the same office: so we, who are many, are one body in Christ, and severally members one of another" (Rom. 12:4, 5). And, again: "But now they are many members, but one body" (1 Cor. 12:20). A body cannot exist without members; at least, the Holy Spirit declares that the church is like a body and has its different members. Such cannot exist without a harmonious functioning of the members. This implies organization. What is it to organize a church? Those who oppose the eldership ought to be able to tell when a church is organized and just when its organization is complete. If a church does not have elders and deacons, what is there about a church that constitutes its organization?

The New Testament clearly teaches the work and duties of the elders. The elders are to "feed the church of the Lord" (Acts 20:28) ; they are to "take heed to all the flock"; they are to govern, or rule, the church; they are to watch in behalf of the souls of its members (Heb. 13:7) ; they are to take the oversight of the church and guide the church in its activities. These with other duties were imposed upon the eldership in New Testament times. Those who dispute these simple declarations must either affirm that all of these duties or work ceased or that this work has been placed upon another class of men. I see no escape from this dilemma. If they claim that the work has ceased and there are no such duties or work needed in the church today, then what are the duties or the work of a church today? Will they claim that no one shall take the oversight of the church, that no one is to govern or to rule the church, that no one should take heed to all the flock and guide the church in its activities? If they take the other horn of the dilemma and say that all of this work is to be done, but another class of members has been designated by the New Testament to do this work then we ask with deep earnestness, Where do we find such instructions in the New Testament? We must know, as they know, that there is not any passage of Scripture in all the New Testament that teaches that the work and duties that the elders in New Testament times did have been transferred to another class of members and that the New Testament church today has no eldership.

Those who make the claim that the eldership has ceased base their claim on the assumption that all elders in the New Testament church were inspired men. This claim is made with great boldness; and since all inspired persons have died and inspiration in its miraculous form has ceased, then all elders have ceased. Is the claim that *all elders in the New Testament were inspired* true? Where is there any Scripture for such a claim? No one can find such a Scripture. In the list of qualifications of elders as mentioned by Paul to Timothy and to Titus, *inspiration is not mentioned as one of the qualifications.* Again, in the list of miraculous gifts mentioned by Paul to the church at Corinth, *elders are not mentioned among them.* Why the omission of inspiration as a qualification, if it was one of the requirements? The qualifications of the elders were mentioned or given to guide in the selection of elders. The selection was to be based upon the qualifications. Since inspiration or a miraculous gift is not mentioned among the qualifications, then we conclude that such was not a requirement.

God's form of government in the early church was vested in the eldership. The elders were to rule well and oversee the church. If elders have ceased or did cease with the miraculous age, did God's form of governing his people cease? If the early form of government for the church ceased, what form of government has been perpetuated, or what form of government does the church have today? Who is divinely appointed to administer this form of government, if indeed, the eldership has ceased? As spiritual gifts were about to disappear we find the eldership was fully established. As the miraculous age was passing, the eldership was established the more firmly or the inspired writers gave instruction as to the kind of men who should be selected to do this work. If the eldership has ceased, then all the qualifications of elders mentioned in the New Testament are of no use to us. That portion of the New Testament which describes the qualifications of elders might as well have been omitted from the New Testament. The Holy Spirit required elders to be appointed in every church. The Holy Spirit never ordained or instructed us that the elders should be discontinued. To discontinue the work of the elders or to discontinue the eldership means to change God's order. One might as well pervert the doctrine and worship of the church as to pervert its organization.

Chapter Six:
THE ELDERSHIP—
THE QUALIFICATIONS

The weighty responsibilities that rest upon the elder-ship necessarily imply high qualifications of character. Any group of men who are vested with the authority to over-see a congregation of saints must be qualified in heart and life to perform such responsible work. Too little attention has been given to the qualifications of elders. The elders themselves have neglected these qualifications and the congregations have oftentimes ignored them. Self-seeking men who desired prominence and preeminence in the church have pushed themselves, with the help of a few politicians, into the position of elders. Only evil can result when such a course has been followed. The time has come when there should be a reformation in the eldership of the congregation. The qualifications as given in the New Tes-tament must not be ignored.

The qualifications of elders are listed in 1 Tim. 3 and Tit. 1. These two lists of the qualifications may be studied with profit by all. They are divided into two classes—the positive qualifications and the negative qualifications. The Holy Spirit has mentioned these qualifications with such emphasis that they cannot be misunderstood. The bishop must be "without reproach," "the husband of one wife," "temperate," "sober-minded," "orderly," "given to hospi-tality," "apt to teach," and "gentle." These are some of the positive characteristics or qualifications of an elder. It is added that he must "rule well his own house" and have a "good report from them that are without." Some of the negative qualifications are that he must be "no brawler,"

31

"no striker," "not contentious," "no lover of money," "not a novice," "not double-tongued," and "not a slanderer." The qualifications as listed in Timothy and Titus vary slightly, but there is no essential difference in these qualifications.

There are very few qualifications listed for the elders which do not belong to all Christians. This shows that the standard for elders is not higher than that for Christians. Sometimes it is argued that no man can attain to the high standard as described by the Holy Spirit in giving the qualifications. The Holy Spirit has never required of man anything that man could not do. God encourages man to measure up to this high standard. It ought to be the goal of every Christian to attain unto such a standard as is described herein. Men were found in New Testament times who met with these requirements. Men who were converted to Christianity from heathenism were soon developed into material for elders; they soon measured up to the high standard outlined by these qualifications. If men converted from idolatry then could attain unto the standard that the Holy Spirit gave for elders, why cannot men who were reared in Christian homes by Christian parents and taught the word of God from their youth up soon develop into elders now? We must conclude that there were men who met these qualifications then, or else the Holy Spirit would not have listed these qualifications and instructed Timothy and Titus to appoint such men as elders. The fact that the eldership was to continue, that it was a permanent feature of the New Testament church, is proof positive that men can attain unto the high standard of the eldership in the church today.

The elders are appointed from the older men. They

come from that class of church members who are settled in their convictions and fixed in their habits of life, and who, if they have yielded to the teachings of Christ, are established in the doctrine of Christ and firm in the faith. If a church follows the teachings of Christ very long, it will soon develop men who are competent to do the work of elders. When Paul and Barnabas made their first missionary tour, they left Antioch and went to Paphos, then to Perga, next to Antioch of Pisidia, then to Iconium, next to Lystra, and then to Derbe. Here they turned around and revisited the churches that had been established. And on their return we read that "when they had appointed for them elders in every church, and had prayed with fasting, they commended them to the Lord, on whom they had believed" (Acts 14:23). These churches where Paul and Barnabas appointed elders were not very old. We cannot determine the time that it took Paul to make his first missionary tour. Many scholars think that it was not longer than three years. None of the churches where he appointed elders at this time were three years old, according to this chronology. The churches at Derbe, Lystra, and Iconium could not have been more than a year old. These churches were composed of some few converted Jews, but a large percentage of them were converted Gentiles. A church composed of converted Jews and Gentiles not older than one year had developed material sufficient to meet the requirement of elders. This argues strongly that such can be done today. No one can claim with assurance that the elders appointed here on this trip were inspired and that they were qualified so quickly by a miraculous gift of the Holy Spirit. Such a position is not tenable.

Some have been discouraged when they understood

the high standard of qualifications of elders and have re-
fused to serve as elders. Such should not be discouraged,
but should strive the harder to measure up to these qualifications. Others have argued that these qualifications
cannot be found in any brother today and that there
should be a number of elders selected, who, combining all
the elders, may have all the qualifications. But the qualifications mentioned should belong to each man. Why
should not a brother have a good report from those who
are without the church? Why should he not so live that
even those who do not accept the Christian religion would
see merit in his character? Why should he not be apt to
teach, temperate, blameless, holy, just, a lover of good,
patient, given to hospitality, sober, vigilant, and a good
husband and father? Why should not every brother control his temper, yield his judgment to others, be a man of
peace, refrain from covetousness, and be free from strong
drink? There are no impossible qualifications of an elder.

When we look at the work of elders and the responsibility that rests upon them, we are not surprised at the
high standard that the Holy Spirit has given for elders. In
fact, if elders are to oversee the flock, they must be men
of sterling qualities and men who have attained unto a
high degree of perfection in Christ Jesus. The wisdom of
God has ordained that men who approach near perfection
in Christ shall be the ones who are directed to take the
oversight of a church. Men who are to feed the flock and
watch after the spiritual interest of all the members of the
church must be men who have a strong faith in God, a
clear conception of the truth, and loyalty to our Lord. Men
who are invested with authority from the Lord Jesus Christ
to rule the Lord's people must be men who love justice,

honor the right, have courage of conviction, and who can control themselves. Men who are selected by the Holy Spirit to discipline the disorderly must be men who are setting the example of orderliness and who watch in the interest of the human soul.

The Eldership of the Churches of Christ

Chapter Seven:
THE ELDERSHIP—ITS DUTIES

The responsibilities of elders are so great that the very best men are required to fill the place. A lack of an efficient eldership which fails to appreciate its responsibilities is a source of much trouble in the congregation. No one who fails to appreciate the work and responsibilities of elders should attempt to fill that place. The duties of elders are clearly outlined in the New Testament Scriptures. No elder need plead ignorance with respect to his duties; no membership need be in doubt as to what are the duties of elders. While the duties are weighty and many, they may be learned from the New Testament.

Paul, in addressing the elders of the church at Ephesus, as recorded in Acts 20:28, instructs them about the duties which they owe to themselves. The first class of duties relates to the elder himself, and the second to the congregation. "Take heed to yourselves" is an admonition which belongs to all Christians, and in a special way it belongs to elders. Elders must see that their own lives must conform to the will of God. Elders should make thorough introspection of their character daily. They should turn the light of God's truth upon their own hearts and see that there is nothing in their hearts that may be displeasing to God. They should spend much time in prayer, and should pray: "Search me, O God, and know my heart: try me, and know my thoughts; and see if there be any wicked way in me, and lead me in the way everlasting" (Ps. 139:23, 24). Elders must be loyal to the Lord and have courage of conviction, and if need be, die rather than prove false to the faith.

Another duty to self is that he must rule well his own house. Elders are chosen from the older men, from men who have families and who have had the experience of training children. If they have trained children to love the Lord, and these children have come into the church through the teachings and training of father, then father is better prepared to train others in the service of God. Truly, "he who knows not how to govern his own family cannot govern a people." The experience of building a home and rearing children in the service of God helps to qualify an elder for the duties of that position. If one has built a home and reared a family in the admonition of the Lord, that one may be better fitted to enter upon a large field of service by taking the oversight with others of the church.

Elders should be sound in the faith; they should hold fast to the faithful word. They should know the truth, love the truth, and be courageous enough to stand for the truth. Their faith should be so strong that no element of doubt ever has disturbed their hearts. They stand related to the congregation as a father to the home, and they must protect it with the same fidelity and courage with which they have protected their own children. At this age elders must protect the flock against false teaching. If they have protected their own children in the education and training of their children against false theories, they are prepared to present the truth in such a way as to defend and protect the members of the church.

Elders are to be examples to the flock. They should realize that they are examples to other members in faith, in purity, in love, in word, and in all manner of living. They are watched closely by other members, and should set such examples as will lead others, when they follow these examples, closer to the Lord Jesus Christ. Peter said, in admonishing elders, that they should not lord "it over the charge allotted" to them, but that they should make themselves "ensamples to the flock" (1 Pet. 5:3).

The second class of duties belonging to elders is their duties to the church. They are to take heed to the flock. They must watch the every need of the flock. Elders should know the congregation and just what it needs. They should know each member of the congregation, and should know the spiritual needs and conditions of each member. Incidentally, it may be said that no congregation should be so large that the eldership cannot know the spiritual needs of every member of it. The elders should know just what progress and development each member has made and should encourage everyone who needs encouragement, as well as instruct those who need instruction. It is one of the duties of the elders to "feed the flock." Nothing is of more importance to the body than the food we eat, and nothing is so important to the church as the spiritual food that is given it. The elders must know that the word of God is taught to each member.

It is the duty of the elders to take the oversight of the congregation. They are to rule well the church of God. "Tend the flock of God which is among you, exercising the oversight, not of constraint, but willingly, according to the will of God" (1 Pet. 5:2). Again: "Let the elders that rule well be counted worthy of double honor, especially those who labor in the word and in teaching" (1 Tim. 5:17). These Scriptures show that the elders are to take the oversight of the church and to discipline it according to the will of God. God has invested the government of his people in the elders of the congregation. All of the authority that Christ has left upon earth for the government of his people has been vested in the elders. Elders must be courageous and faithful in performing their duty in disciplining the church. There should be a united effort on the part of the elders to direct the affairs of the church in such a way that the greatest good may be done, and this can be done only by carrying out the will of the Lord. The church is not a democracy in which all the members have an equal voice in directing the affairs. The church of our Lord is ruled, when the will of God is carried out, by the Head of the church, which is Christ. He rules through the eldership.

Elders are not to be tyrants. They are not to be cruel and heartless, lording it over God's people, but they are to be as fathers, with wise heads and loving hearts ruling the Lord's people. Somebody must take the lead; someone must direct the work; someone must carry out the discipline of the congregation. These duties belong to the elders. There are duties which the congregation owes to the elders. When the Holy Spirit teaches elders to rule over the congregation, it at the same time teaches the congregation to submit to the government of the elders. When God commands someone to teach, there is an equal command to the one taught to learn. So, when God teaches the elders to rule over the congregation, at the same time he teaches the congregation to submit to the government of the elders. Therefore, the Holy Spirit says to the congregation: "Remember them that had the rule over you, men that spake unto you the word of God; and considering the issue of their life, imitate their faith" (Heb. 13:7; see, also, verse 17).

Elders are to rule, teach, and exercise discipline in the

church. They are to teach the word of God, or feed the flock with the sincere milk of the word They must not only preserve the word of God intact, but they must resist the introduction of innovations. The congregation is to honor them as fathers, obey them as God's shepherds, receive not an accusation against them except at the mouth of two or more witnesses, count them worthy of double honor, and imitate their faith.

Chapter Eight:
THE ELDERSHIP AND PREACHERS

If we will study the conditions that now exist in the churches of Christ, we must conclude that there is a need for a restoration of the New Testament order of both elders and preachers. It is as important to maintain the New Testament order of organization in the church as it is to maintain the faith and worship of the church. The practice of churches' employing preachers to give full time to the church is rapidly increasing. We are developing a serious condition in the churches.

Preachers are called upon to make all the public addresses, to make the announcements and plan the program of the church; they are called upon to look after the flock in their private activities, preach funerals, and perform marriage ceremonies. The preacher is more popular and has more influence in the church than have the elders. God placed the guidance, teaching, discipline, and the development of the church under the eldership of the church. When the preacher gains the confidence and esteem of the church and has greater influence over the membership than do the elders, there is something wrong. It has been known that preachers have gone to establish congregations, and they got the control of the congregation within six months' time, and ousted, by popular vote, the elders of the church who had been serving the church for many years. Preachers are usurping authority and lording it over the church until the eldership has become a nonentity in the church. The preacher has exalted himself and has usurped authority until he reigns over the church like a pope. When the eldership displeases the

43

preacher, some excuse is found for displacing the elder and electing someone to take his place who will do the bidding of the preacher. Is the preacher amenable to the eldership? Must the elders submit to the preacher? In some places the preachers have openly declared that the eldership is inferior to the preacher; that the preacher is above the eldership.

We use the word "preacher" for the New Testament word "evangelist." The Greek word "*evaggelistees*," translated "evangelist," denotes a gospel preacher. It occurs only three times in the New Testament. (1) Acts 21:8. Paul and his company came to Caesarea and there entered "into the house of Philip, the evangelist, who was one of the seven" (2) 2 Tim. 4:5. Here Paul exhorts Timothy to "suffer hardship, do the work of an evangelist, fulfill thy ministry" (3) Eph. 4:11. "And he gave some to be apostles; and some, prophets; and some, evangelists; and some, pastors and teachers." These are the only occurrences of the word from which we get "evangelist." These instances show that the evangelist was the one who preached the glad tidings, and had no reference whatever to any official class. This did not mean to deliver religious orations or merely to sermonize as we see done today. It signified the labor of turning the hearts of the people from sin to God by teaching the truth as it is revealed in Christ Jesus. The evangelist showed that those in sin were lost and that the love of God had given Jesus Christ as a ransom for those in bondage to sin.

Another duty of the evangelist was to gather those who had believed on the Lord, who had repented of their sins, and who had been baptized into Christ, into one group and thus organize them into a church. Those who were converted needed to be developed; they needed to be fed on the sincere milk of the word and taught how to live the Christian life. A large part of the work of evangelists consisted in teaching the young converts and developing men who would take the oversight of the congregation. Preachers have sermonized and can make "talks" or speeches on Bible subjects, but cannot train young converts in the work of the Lord. Truly, there is an incompetency in many preachers, or evangelists. We need wiser and better workers in the vineyard of the Lord. The churches and the world need men who can "do the work of an evangelist." Churches often fail to purify the heart and educate the members up to the spiritual standard of efficiency in Christ Jesus. This failure is due in part to the inefficiency of preachers.

Another duty of the evangelist was to set in order all things that were wanting in the churches and to see that each member was busy in the place which his qualifications assigned him. The care of the churches in the early day rested upon the evangelist. Paul and Barnabas, Timothy and Titus, and all others not only preached the gospel and broadcast the seed of the kingdom, but they felt a great anxiety for the churches of Christ. Preachers today ought to be interested in a general way in the churches of Christ. In some cities the preachers are interested in getting members from other congregations. In some places daily invitations are given to the people of God by the preacher to come and build up that particular congregation. Many preachers selfishly wish to build up "their church" to make a show and appear to be doing a wonderful work. Such is not the work of an evangelist.

The work of an evangelist is under the eldership of the

church. If an evangelist goes to a place to labor for a week or for a year with that church, he ought to recognize the eldership and work under the supervision of the elders. It is true that there is a great deficiency in the eldership of all the churches; it is true that possibly none of the elders measure up to the standard of the New Testament requirements; but it is also true that evangelists are as inefficient and imperfect as are the elders. The incompetency of the eldership does not justify the evangelist in perverting God's order of organization. The preacher has no more right to disturb or pervert the New Testament order of the organization of the church than he has to pervert the faith or corrupt the worship of the church. For a preacher to rebel against the Scriptural eldership of the church is to rebel against God and his order of organization. It is a high crime against God for the preacher to usurp the authority of the eldership and by popular applause lead the membership away from the Scriptural order of the organization of the church.

If the evangelist understands the New Testament teaching, he will understand that his is not an office, but a work. Many have been led to think that all preachers are "elders," and many think that preachers are "pastors." "Elder," "overseer," "presbyter," "bishop," and "pastor" are different names for the same class. A preacher might be an elder, but he is not an elder simply because he preaches. It is a perversion of God's order to speak of the preacher as "the pastor." He may not even be *a* pastor, and surely he cannot be *the* pastor. It is the custom of some preachers to get themselves appointed as an elder of the congregation where they go. Oftentimes the preacher is the chairman of the "board of elders," thus

placing
the eldership of the church under the preacher. There can be success in the church only as it follow God's order in organization as well as in faith and worship. A leader or preacher who perverts the organization of the church corrupts even its worship.

Chapter Nine:
THE ELDERSHIP AND DISCIPLINE

One of the important duties of the eldership is that of overseeing or ruling the congregation. The elders were instructed to oversee the flock, keep it in order, settle the difficulties that arise, and enforce the laws of God. It is clearly understood that the elders have no power or authority, save that which has been vested in them by the Lord Jesus Christ. They have no power to legislate or enact laws for the church, neither do they have any power to release that which the Lord has made binding upon his church. Elders have no choice in the matter of ruling the church; they have no power to change the doctrine of Christ or the worship of the church. They are to enforce the rule of God over his people. They must be as faithful in enforcing the rule of God as they are in teaching the will of God. This calls for discipline.

The elders have been made the rulers, overseers, mouthpieces of God to his people in all dispensations of God to man. The elders are the ones through whom God decides cases and enforces his laws in the church. God has never, in any age, left the decisions of questions and difficulties that arise among his people to the vote of majorities. The majority vote includes the young, the thoughtless, the untaught, the inexperienced, and the incompetent to decide such important matters. Such a course as this would be to govern the church by impulse, favor, passion, prejudice, and not by the law of God. Even our civil powers do not decide the guilt by popular majority. God decides all questions in his kingdom. In the church he has ordained to rule his people through the eldership. The

Scriptural eldership, acting according to the law of God, has the full authority of God to discipline the disorderly. The New Testament is the law of the church, and the elders are the Scriptural representatives of God to enforce this law according to the will of God.

Elders have no authority from God to rule or act for any church, save that one of which they are members and over which the Holy Spirit has made them bishops. There is no New Testament precedent of elders extending their authority over any one who is not a member of the church over which these elders are appointed. The discipline that may be administered belongs to the membership of the church and to no other membership. Each church with its Scriptural eldership, acting Scripturally, is the highest authority in the government of God's people here on earth. No association, conference, convention, or any other human authority has any divine right to exercise discipline over a member of the church. Only the church through its eldership has authority over members of the church. There is no God-appointed tribunal to which a member of the church may appeal after a Scriptural eldership has Scripturally administered discipline to any disorderly member.

The moment any elder or set of elders begin to extend their authority or discipline over others than members of their own congregation, that moment they cease to act as God's representatives upon earth. The decisions and rulings and discipline of the eldership of a church belong only to that church, and other churches are free before God to act upon matters which pertain to their own congregation. It is true that the standards of righteous living are the same in all the churches that follow the New Testament;

it is also true that the principles of discipline given in the New Testament belong to all of the churches; but it is not true that the decisions and discipline of one set of elders must be enforced upon another church, simply because the eldership of the first church so acted.

God has not tied together the churches of Christ through the discipline or actions of the eldership. It is the duty of the elders of the church to see that a thorough investigation of every case that comes up is made. It is not only the duty of the elders to investigate, but it is their duty to direct the investigation and see that it is just, full, and fair. This investigation does not necessarily have to be made before the boys and girls of the congregation. The discreet and prudent men of experience ought to investigate prayerfully the case and put it in such form that every member of the church will be satisfied of the justice of the decision. Brother D. Lipscomb wrote on this point as follows: "It is utterly impossible that men and women can act earnestly and heartily in a church when they believe it guilty of injustice and wrong to its members. An eldership that assumes such authority assumes to be the church and lords it over God's heritage. *An eldership that refuses to satisfy by investigation a single member of the church proves its unfitness and incompetency to rule a congregation of disciples of Christ"* (The italics are by the writer and are given for emphasis).

A fearful responsibility rests upon the elders in exercising discipline. It takes true courage on the part of elders to enforce the will of God in cases of discipline. Elders cannot become a party to strife or to a difficulty. The moment that elders become a party to any difficulty in the church, that moment they disqualify themselves to act as God's representatives in the discipline. Even in our civil courts no juror, witness, or judge can act without bias upon a case to which he is a party. When trouble arises in the congregation, the elders must see that they do not become parties to the matter; they are to keep themselves free from any bias or prejudice or personalities in the affair. After the investigation has been made with prayerfulness and thoroughness, then the matter is presented to the congregation, and every member of the congregation must act Scripturally and carry out the will of God. It is as much the duty of the members of the church to carry out the will of God as it is the eldership. No intelligent, Scriptural eldership will put a matter before the church in such a way as to call for those who are in favor of the exclusion or retention of the disorderly. The question to be decided is whether or not the law of God has been violated and whether all Scriptural procedures of discipline have been made.

No man on earth is infallible; no set of men is infallible. The eldership and the entire church are made up of fallible beings. It is presumption on the part of the eldership or a church to assume that its actions are infallible. This is why God has placed the responsibility upon each church to decide matters of its own. A congregation may with courtesy examine the findings of another congregation when that matter has been pressed upon it, but it is under no obligation to accept *in toto* the decisions of another congregation. There is no principle taught in the New Testament that enforces the decision of one eldership or church upon that of another. The wrongs or mistakes of one church must not bind others to the same mistakes; neither must the right decisions of one church bind another church to those rights. The church must act on its own initiative, exercising its own autonomy in all of these matters. Discipline is such a serious matter that elders and churches must act according to the will of God, or else the action becomes a usurpation of the authority of God and a perversion of the will of God.

Chapter Ten:
THE ELDERSHIP—SOME QUESTIONS

Sometimes questions help to clear a subject in that they call for some straight thinking. Many questions about the eldership need to be considered and answered in order that the subject may be viewed from every angle. Again, sometimes questions need to be asked because the minds of many are confused on the subject, and a question helps to clear the confusion away. Sometimes questions are asked in order to confuse. Paul admonished Timothy: "But foolish and ignorant questionings refuse, knowing that they gender strifes" (2 Tim. 2:23). We will consider only such questions as will throw light on the subject of New Testament teaching on the eldership.

When is a church organized?

When a group of Christians is meeting in a place for worship and doing all that the Lord requires of a church to do. A church as viewed by the New Testament is a body. When all of the members of the body are working and worshiping in the name of the Lord, the church is organized. It is organized when the elders and deacons are appointed and are directing the members according to the will of God.

Can a church worship God acceptably without Scripturally qualified elders? If so, how long can it do so?

A church is a church only when it is fully organized. It cannot be properly termed a "church" in its completeness until it has all of the essential qualities of a New Testament church. A church that is filling its mission or is in the process of development may please God without or before it has elders; but if it is developing as rapidly as is possible, it will not be long until there will be material ready to take the oversight of the congregation. The question means, how long will it take for a group of newborn babes in Christ to arrive at the point where there will be members qualified to take the lead? Surely no church could be pleasing to the Lord when it has stopped or ceased to develop its membership. No church ought to want to remain in the undeveloped and incomplete state. It ought to press on to its full capacity in its full development. Some churches in the New Testament were ready for elders within a short time.

Can elders resign? How long should they serve? Can they be ousted?

Let us ask, *Can a Christian resign?* No one can resign from any work which he is qualified to do and still be pleasing to the Lord. If a brother is Scripturally qualified to serve as an elder, then he cannot resign from that which he is Scripturally qualified to do. As to the length of time that one should serve as an elder, it seems that he should serve as long as he is qualified to serve. Some grow old and feeble and become inactive; some may become unfit by loss of mental powers or physical strength; but so long as one is qualified and active for the work of an elder, so long should that one serve as an elder. When an elder who is qualified resigns, he resigns the work of God.

No; a Scripturally qualified elder cannot be ousted by those who are doing the will of the Lord. "Against an elder receive not an accusation, except at the mouth of two or three witnesses" (1 Tim. 5:19). If the members of the church should oust an elder who is Scripturally qualified and who is Scripturally functioning as an elder, then the ones ousting him are rebelling against God's authority and God's work. If an elder is unfaithful in life and in his teaching and ruling, he is thereby disqualified as an elder.

How many elders are necessary for a Scripturally organized church?

The New Testament, in referring to elders, always uses the plural number. "Elders" were appointed in every church. Hence, for a church to be Scripturally organized with elders, there must be a plurality of elders. The size of the congregation would help to determine the number of elders. Large congregations need a greater number of elders than do the smaller churches.

If one does not have all of the qualifications, but has more than half of them, can that one be an elder?

It would be difficult to find a brother who has only part of the qualifications of elders. The qualifications are such that they become traits of character, or they are such that very few of them can be possessed singly or alone. The life that develops some of the qualifications will develop many if not all of them.

If all of the brethren in a church have all of the qualifications, would all of them be elders? If not, who would have the right to say who should serve as elders?

These questions are hypothetical. The elders are taken

from the older and more experienced men of the church. It is not probable that all of these members of a church that is filling its mission would be old men. It is not probable that the lives lived that develop the qualifications of elders would not constantly be bringing into the church new converts. If one functions as an elder, that one will be teaching others and converting others. At any rate, the elders in New Testament times were appointed. They were appointed by an evangelist or by the congregation. When the elders were *appointed,* the other members would know who the elders were. The appointment was a way of designating those who should take the lead or oversight of the church.

Do elders have authority over members of other churches? Can a brother be an elder over more than one church?

Elders have only such authority as is vested in them by the Lord. The Lord has not given any authority to an elder, except over the church of which he is a member. No elder can by the authority of the Lord extend his power or authority over any other congregation. Such a condition would destroy the autonomy of the local congregation. No brother can be an elder over more than one church at a time. The duties of an elder are such that his whole time will be taken by the congregation of which he is a member. Again, if one could be an elder of two or more churches, that would destroy the autonomy of the church and would tie the different churches together under one human head. The Lord never intended that a brother be an elder of more than one church at a time.

How did the Holy Spirit make elders? How does the Holy Spirit make elders today?

Paul instructed Timothy and Titus to appoint elders. Paul and Barnabas appointed elders. Paul was guided by the Holy Spirit in writing to Timothy and Titus. When these evangelists followed the instructions of the Holy Spirit, it was the Holy Spirit appointing elders. The Holy Spirit makes elders today just as he makes Christians. The Holy Spirit makes Christians with the preaching of the gospel and obedience to the gospel. When one does what the Holy Spirit teaches, that one is guided by the Holy Spirit, whether that be in becoming a Christian or in doing any phase of the work of the church. In addressing the elders of the church at Ephesus, Paul said to them: "Take heed unto yourselves, and to all the flock, in which the Holy Spirit hath made you bishops, to feed the church of the Lord which he purchased with his own blood" (Acts 20:28). The Holy Spirit had made these men elders through Paul or some other servant of God. So the Holy Spirit makes elders of men today.